TOP of the CHARTS

The best of the 00s

Amazed | 05
Lonestar

Back To Black | 10
Amy Winehouse

Black And Gold | 22
Sam Sparro

Bleeding Love | 16
Leona Lewis

The Climb | 32
Miley Cyrus

Come Away With Me | 27
Norah Jones

Crazy | 36
Gnarls Barkley

Dare | 42
Gorillaz

Eternity | 50
Robbie Williams

Fallin' | 60
Alicia Keys

The Fear | 66
Lily Allen

Fight For This Love | 55
Cheryl Cole

Fill My Little World | 70
The Feeling

Handbags And Gladrags | 76
Stereophonics

Haven't Met You Yet | 81
Michael Bublé

How To Save A Life | 96
The Fray

Howl | 88
Florence & The Machine

Hung Up | 103
Madonna

110	**I Don't Feel Like Dancin'** Scissor Sisters
118	**Last Request** Paolo Nutini
124	**Life For Rent** Dido
134	**One Day Like This** Elbow
129	**Over The Rainbow** Eva Cassidy
140	**Patience** Take That
146	**Pyramid Song** Radiohead
150	**Rockstar** Nickelback
164	**Sound Of The Underground** Girls Aloud
156	**Strange And Beautiful** Aqualung
160	**Sweet About Me** Gabriella Cilmi
169	**Talk** Coldplay
176	**These Words** Natasha Bedingfield
182	**Valerie** Mark Ronson feat. Amy Winehouse
187	**Wake Me Up When September Ends** Green Day
192	**Warwick Avenue** Duffy
199	**You Raise Me Up** Westlife
204	**You're Beautiful** James Blunt

© 2010 by Faber Music Ltd
First published by Faber Music Ltd in 2010
Bloomsbury House 74–77 Great Russell Street
London WC1B 3DA

Edited by Lucy Holliday
Designed by Lydia Merrills-Ashcroft
Additional Photos © Getty Images

Printed in England by Caligraving Ltd
All rights reserved

The text paper used in this publication is a virgin fibre
product that is manufactured in the UK to ISO 14001
standards. The wood fibre used is only sourced from
managed forests using sustainable forestry principles.
This paper is 100% recyclable

ISBN10:0-571-53339-6
EAN13:978-0-571-53339-8

To buy Faber Music publications or to find out about the full
range of titles available, please contact your local music retailer
or Faber Music sales enquiries:

Faber Music Ltd, Burnt Mill, Elizabeth Way,
Harlow, CM20 2HX England
Tel:+44(0)1279 82 89 82 Fax:+44(0)1279 82 89 83
sales@fabermusic.com fabermusic.com

AMAZED

Words and Music by Marv Green, Aimee Mayo and Chris Lindsey

1. Ev-'ry time our eyes meet, this feel-ing in - side me is al-most more than I can
2. The smell of your skin, the taste of your kiss, the way you whis - per in the

BACK TO BLACK

Words and Music by Amy Winehouse and Mark Ronson

BLEEDING LOVE

Words and Music by Jesse McCartney and Ryan Tedder

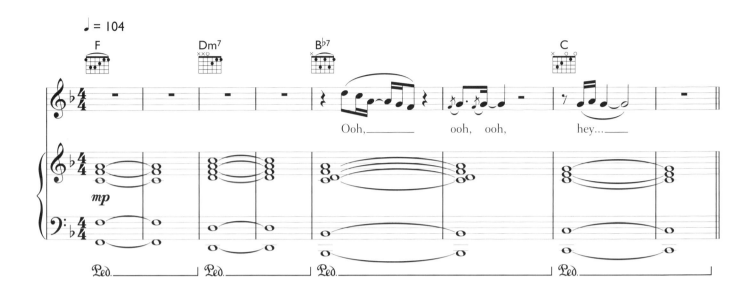

Ooh,_____   ooh, ooh,   hey..._____

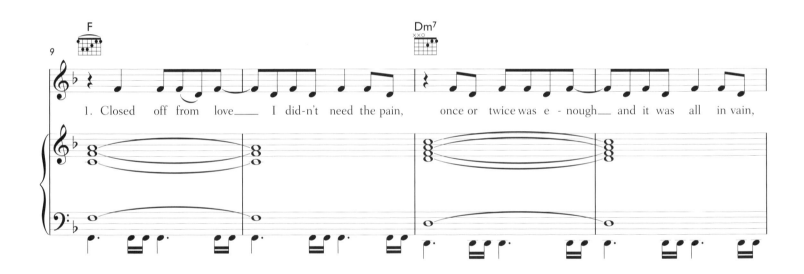

1. Closed   off from love____ I did-n't need the pain,   once or twice was e - nough___ and it was   all   in vain,

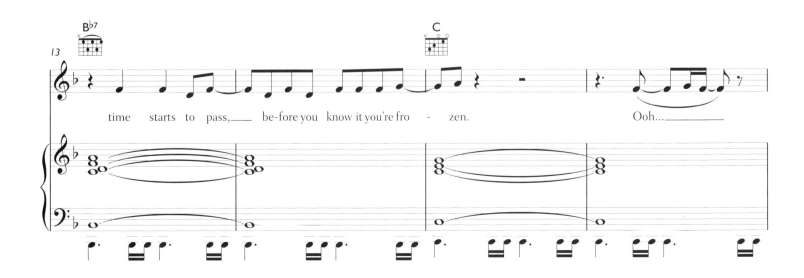

time   starts to pass,____ be-fore you know it you're fro - zen.   Ooh..._____

I don't care what they say, I'm in love___ with you, they try to pull me a-way but they don't know the truth,

my heart's crip-pled by the vein that I keep on clos - ing, ooh,___ you cut me o-pen and I___

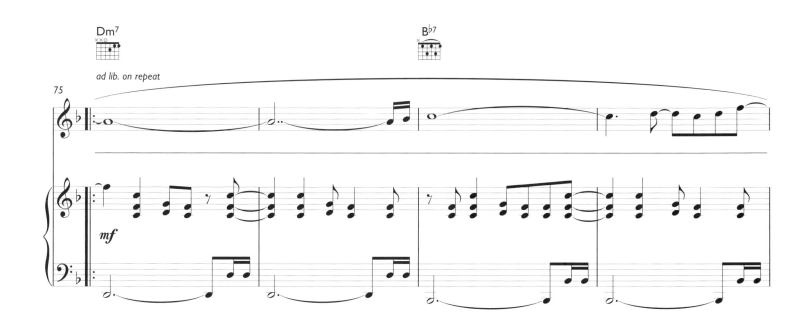

ad lib. on repeat

BLACK AND GOLD

Words and Music by Jesse Rogg and Samuel Falson

COME AWAY WITH ME

Words and Music by Norah Jones

And I_____ want to wake up_____ with the rain_____ fall - ing on a tin_____ roof,

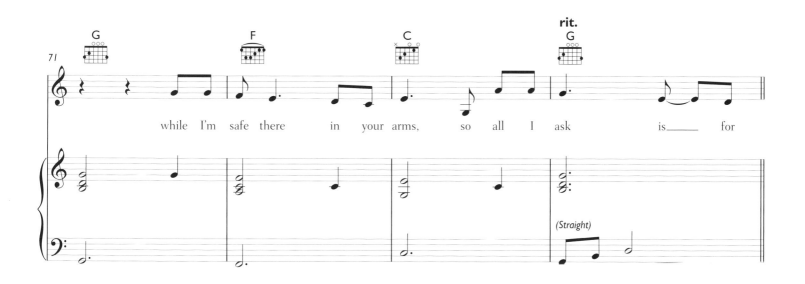

while I'm safe there in your arms, so all I ask is_____ for

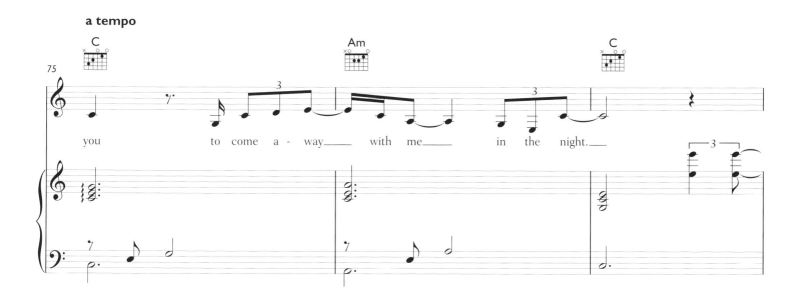

you to come a - way_____ with me_____ in the night._____

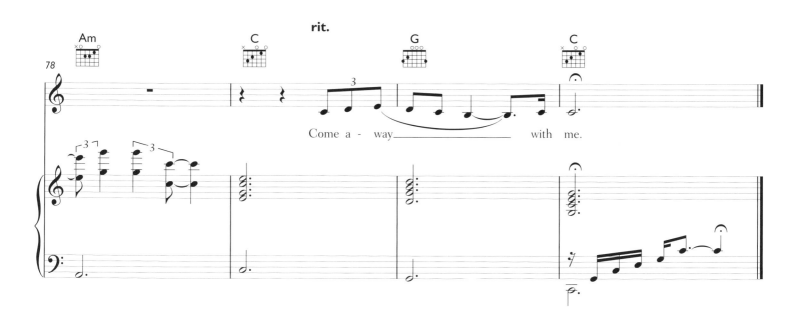

Come a - way_____ with me.

THE CLIMB

Words and Music by Jessica Alexander and Jon Mabe

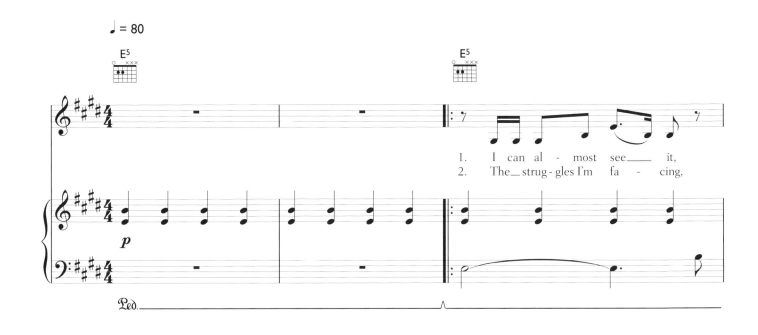

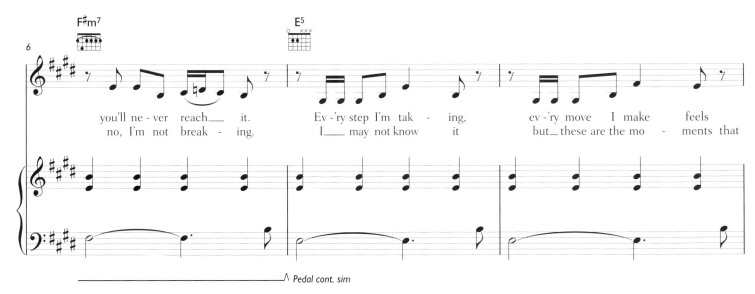

CRAZY

Words and Music by Thomas Callaway, Brian Burton,
Gianfranco Reverberi and Gian Piero Reverberi

Does that make me cra - - zy?_____ Pos - sib - ly.___

2. And I hope that you_ are hav -
3. My he - roes had the heart_

- ing_ the time_ of_ your life,_____ but think twice;
___ to lose their lives out on a limb,_____ and all I re-mem-

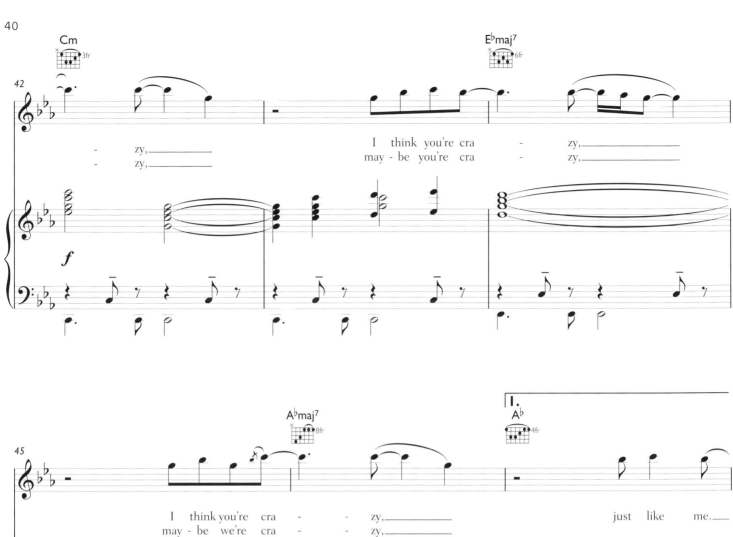

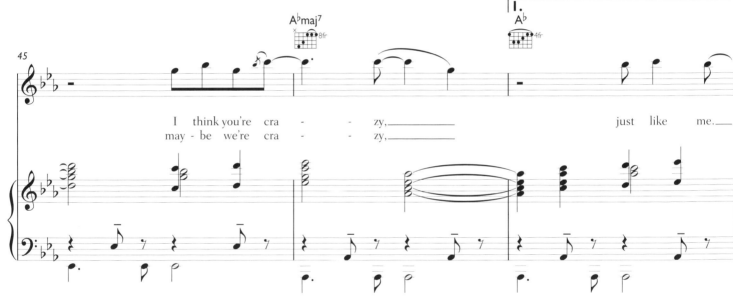

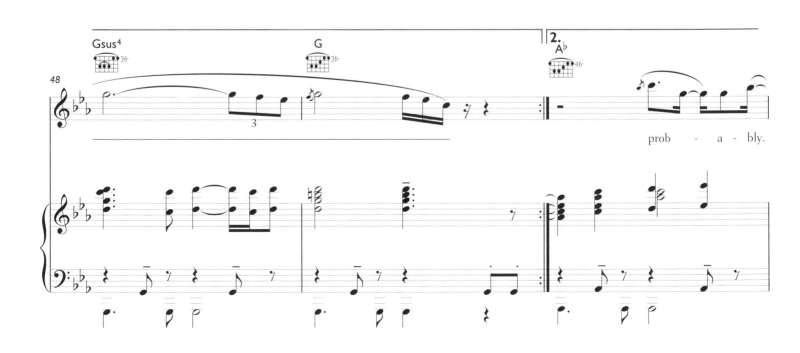

DARE

Words and Music by Gorillaz and Dangermouse

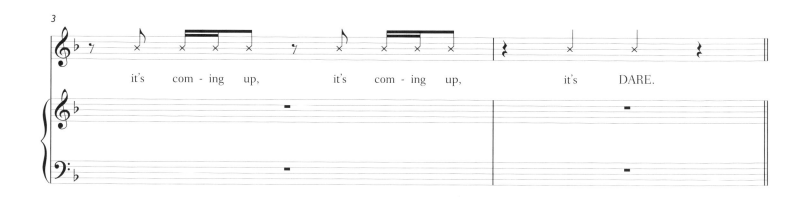

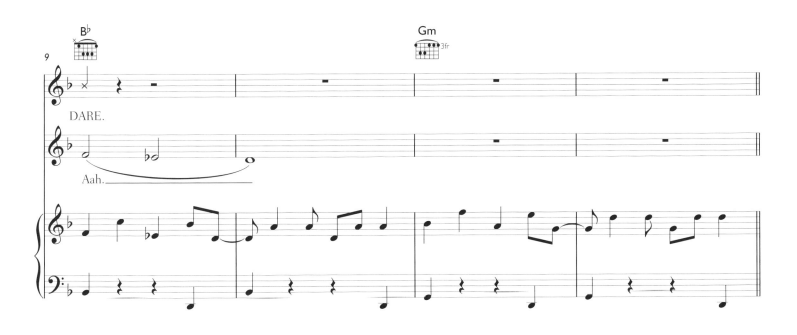

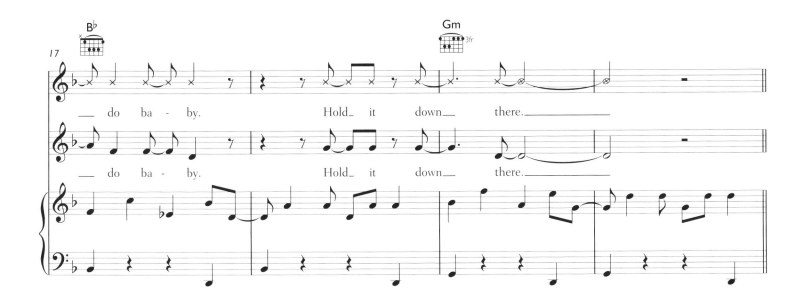

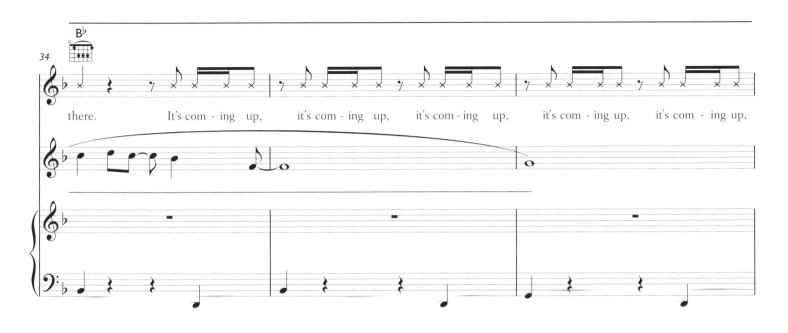

there.   It's com - ing up,   it's com - ing up,   it's com - ing up,   it's com - ing up,   it's com - ing up,

it's there.   It's

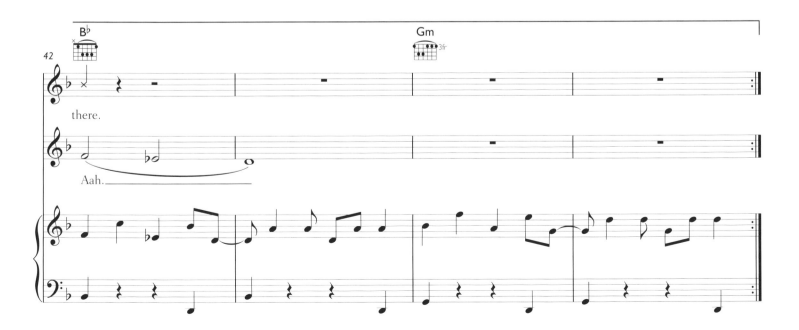

there.

Aah.

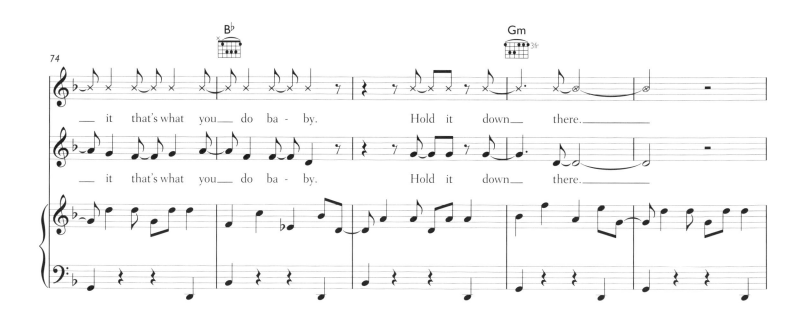

were there_ your-self,___ work_ it_____ out._____

were there_ your-self,___ work_ it_____ out._____

Ooh._____

ETERNITY

Words and Music by Robert Williams and Guy Chambers

FIGHT FOR THIS LOVE

Words and Music by Stephen Kipner, Wayne Wilkins and Andre Merritt

FALLIN'

Words and Music by Alicia Augello-Cook

THE FEAR

Words and Music by Lily Allen and Greg Kurstin

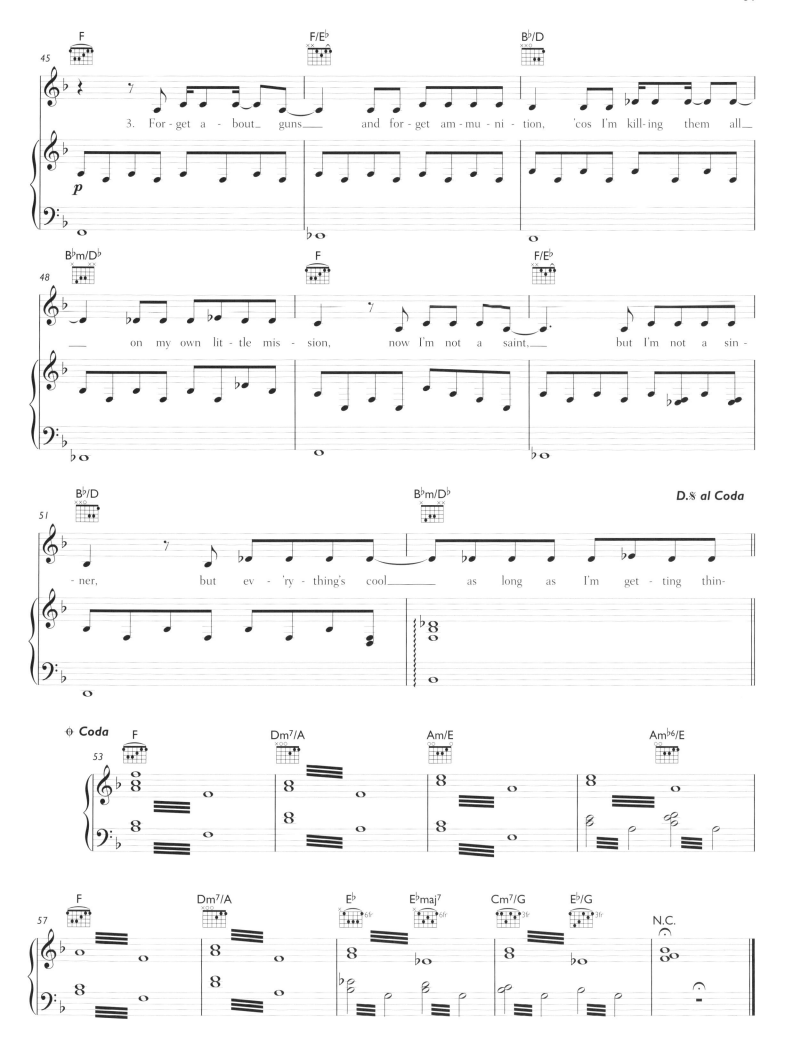

FILL MY LITTLE WORLD

Words and Music by Dan Gillespie Sells and The Feeling

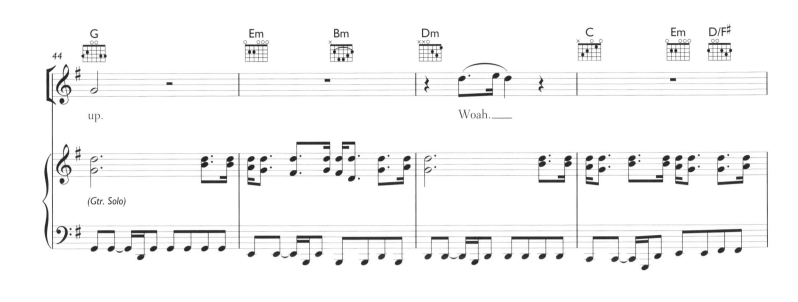

up.   Woah.____

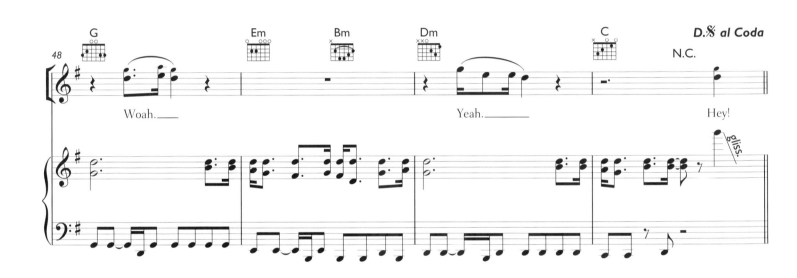

Woah.____   Yeah._____   Hey!

up, right   up.   Hey!   Show some love,__ you   ain't so__ tough, come   fill my lit - tle world right

HANDBAGS AND GLADRAGS

Words and Music by Michael D'Abo

They told me you missed school_____ to - day,__

so what I sug-gest you just   throw them all__ a- way,__   the hand-bags and the glad - rags that your poor__

__ old Gran-dad had to sweat to buy__ you,   woh,__ woh._____

They told me you missed

HAVEN'T MET YOU YET

Words and Music by Michael Bublé, Alan Chang and Amy Foster-Gillies

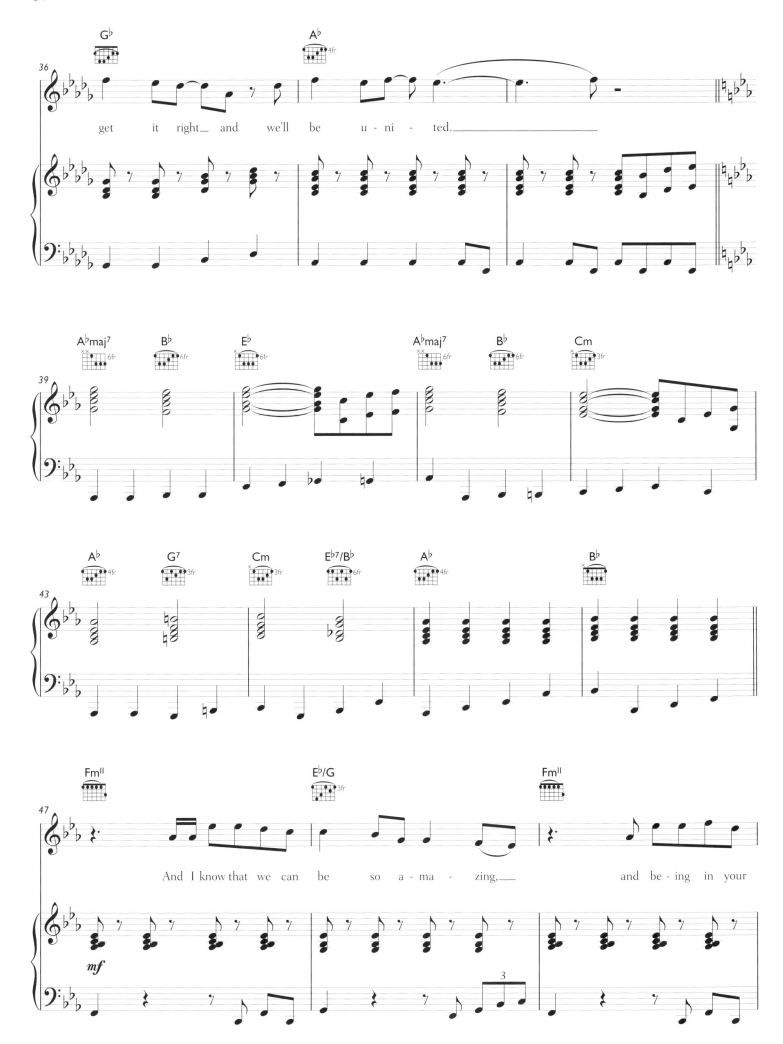

get it right__ and we'll be u - ni - ted._____

And I know that we can be so a - ma - zing,___ and be - ing in your

HOWL

Words and Music by Florence Welch and Paul Epworth

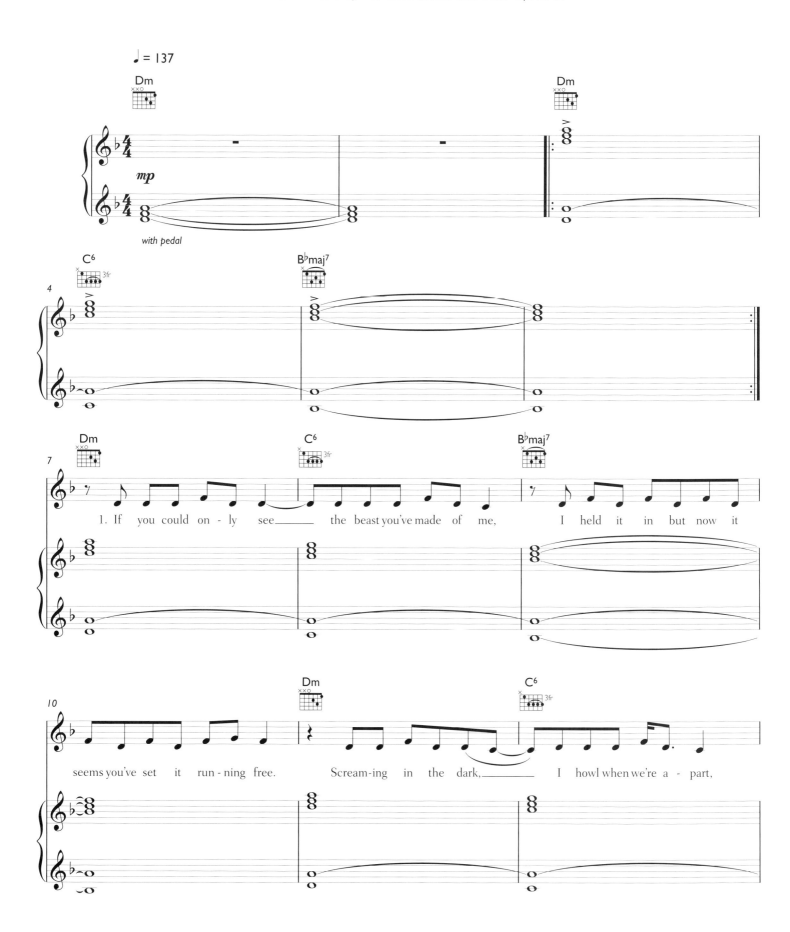

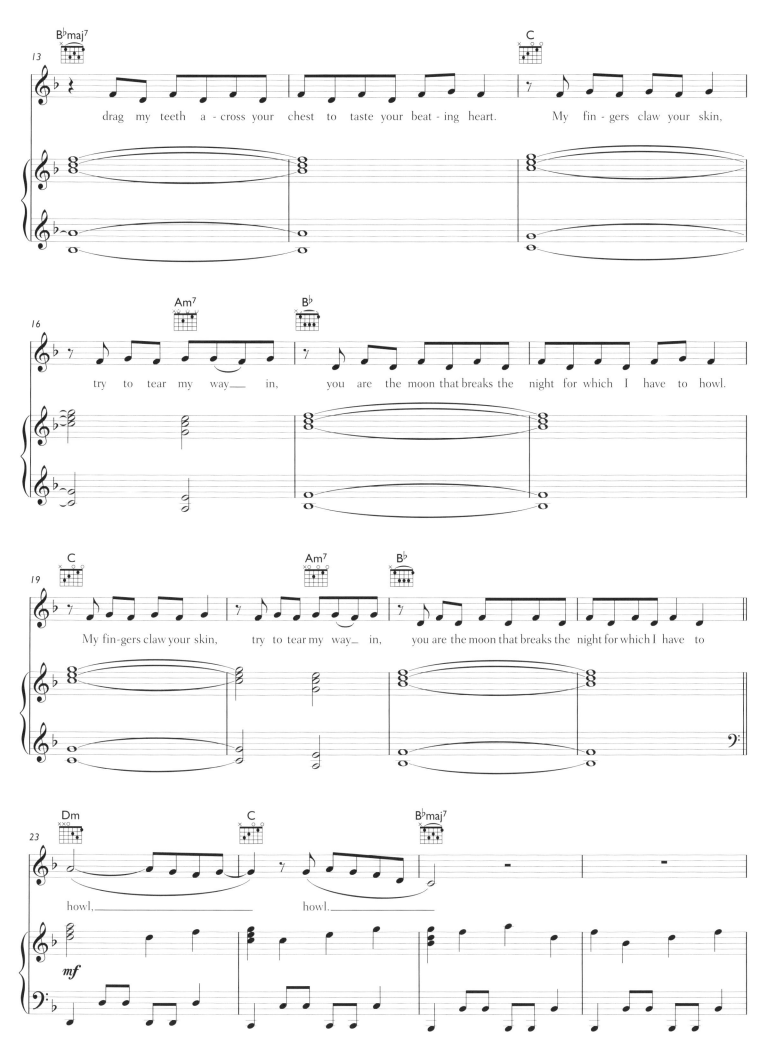

HOW TO SAVE A LIFE

Words and Music by Joseph King and Isaac Slade

HUNG UP

Words and Music by Madonna, Stuart Price,
Benny Andersson and Björn Ulvaeus

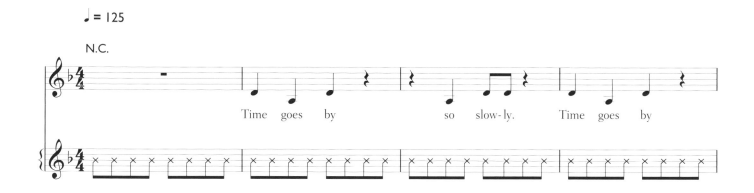

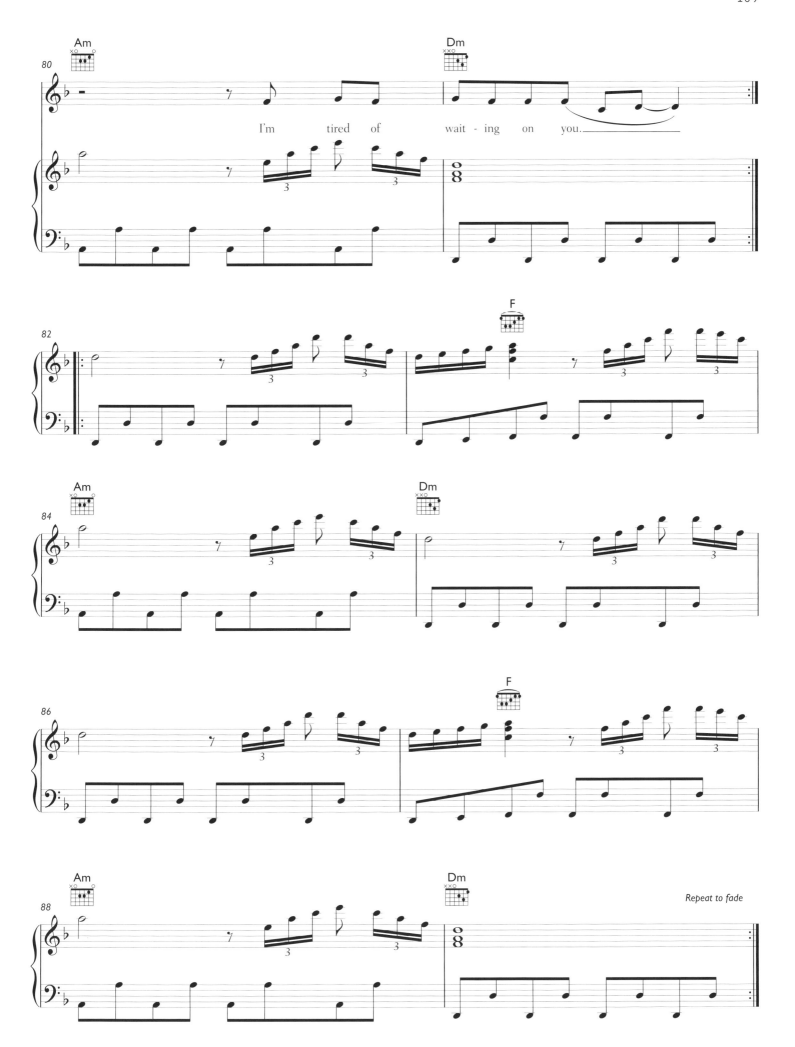

I DON'T FEEL LIKE DANCIN'

Words and Music by Scott Hoffman, Jason Sellards and Elton John

You＿ can't make me dance＿

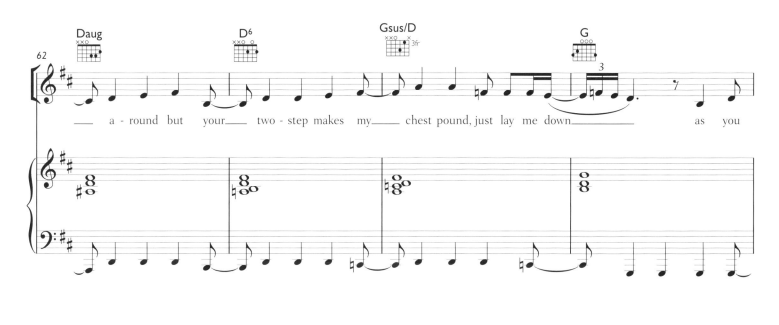

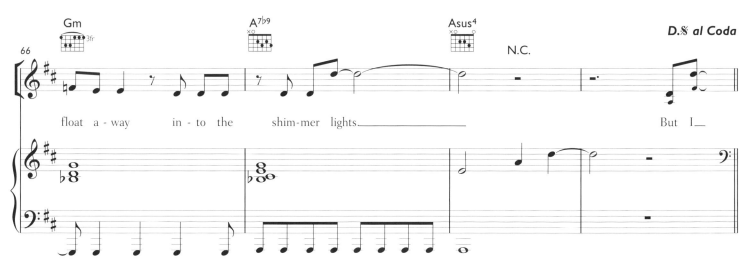

LAST REQUEST

Words and Music by Paolo Giovanni Nutini, Jim Duguid, Matt Benbrook,
Annunzio Paolo Mantovani, Stephen Foster and Nikolai Andrej Rimsky-Korsakoff

120

LIFE FOR RENT

Words and Music by Dido Armstrong and Rollo Armstrong

heart is a shield, and I won't let it down.

While I am so a - fraid to fail,

so I won't e - ven try.

Well how can I say I'm a - live? But if my

D.%. al Coda

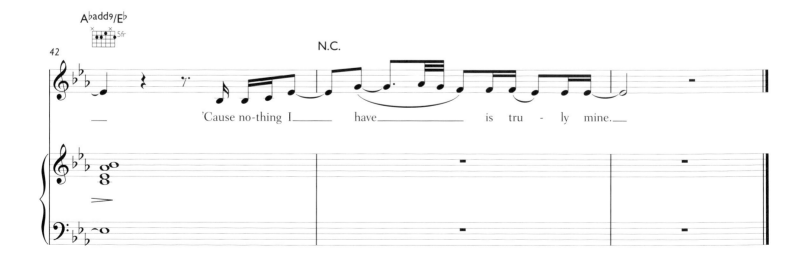

OVER THE RAINBOW

(FROM "THE WIZARD OF OZ")

Music by Harold Arlen
Lyrics by E Y Harburg

131

ONE DAY LIKE THIS

Words and Music by Guy Garvey, Craig Potter, Mark Potter, Peter Turner and Richard Jupp

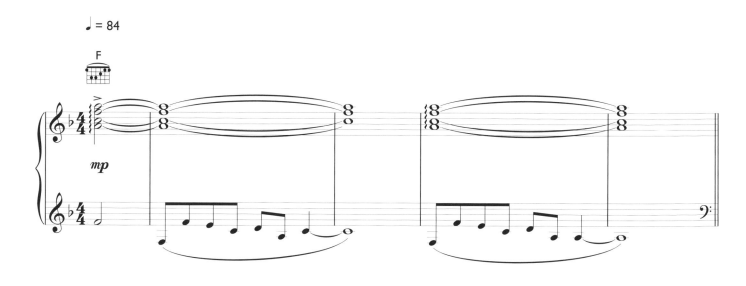

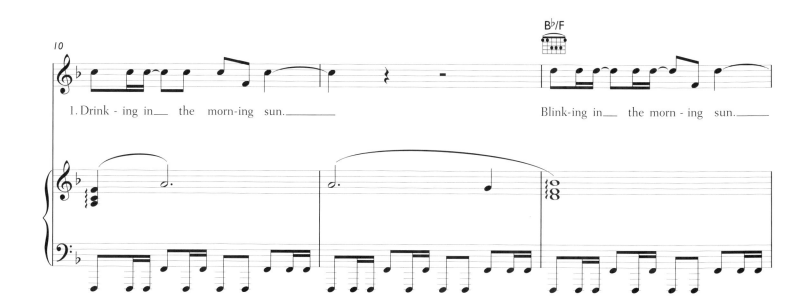

1. Drink - ing in___ the morn - ing sun._____

Blink - ing in___ the morn - ing sun._____

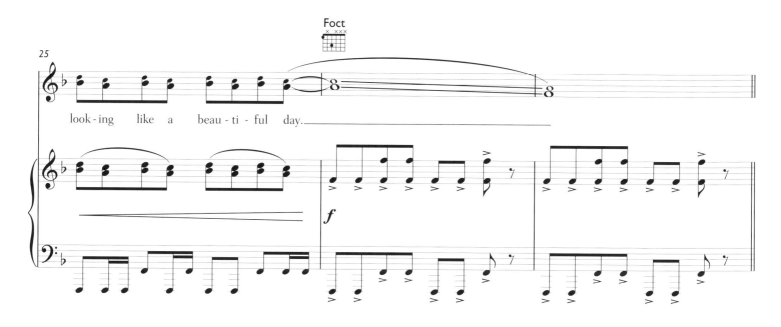

PATIENCE

Words and Music by Howard Donald, Jason Orange,
Gary Barlow, Mark Owen and John Shanks

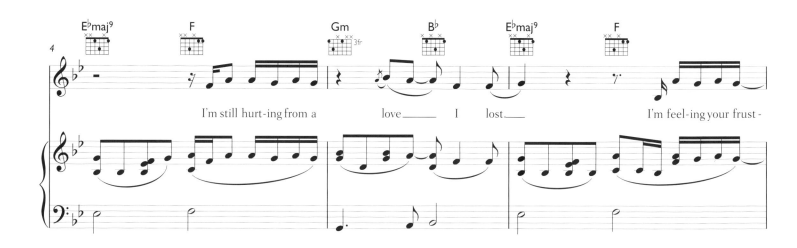

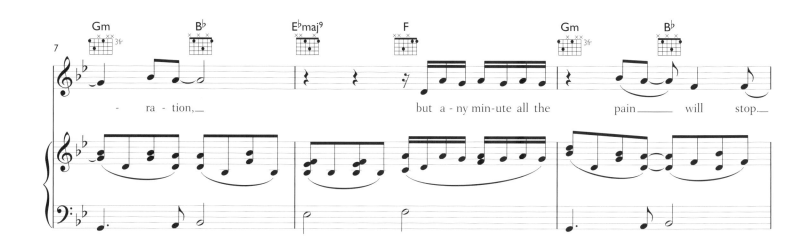

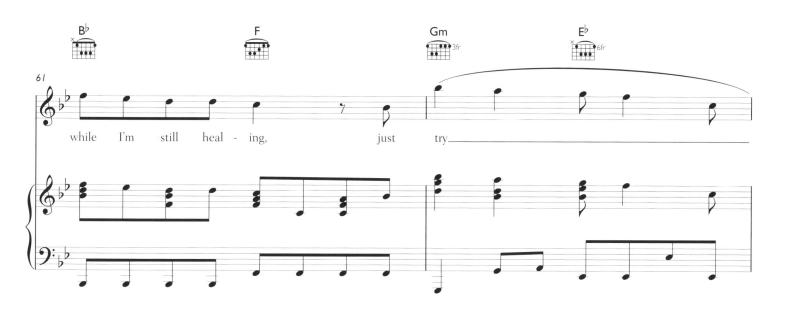

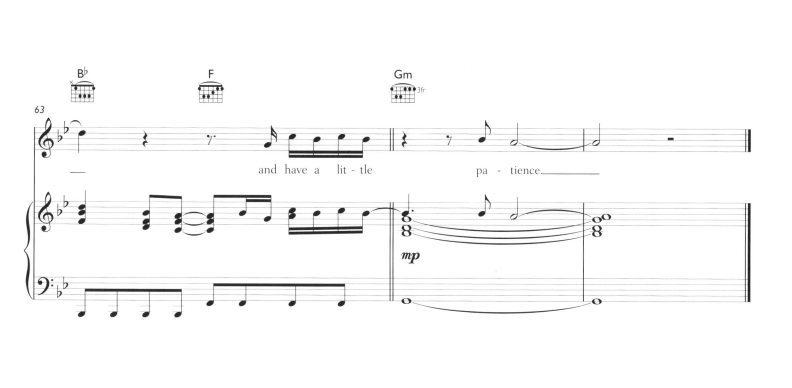

PYRAMID SONG

Words and Music by Thomas Yorke, Jonathan Greenwood,
Edward O'Brien, Philip Selway and Colin Greenwood

Ooh,_____   ooh,_____

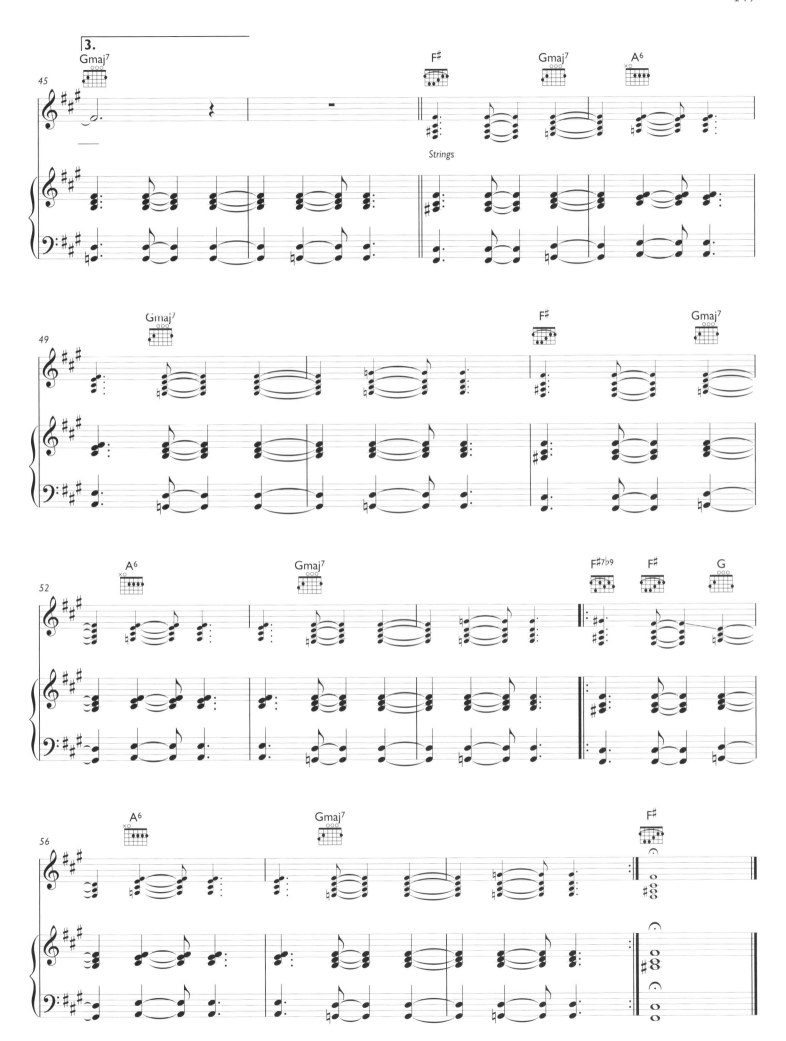

ROCK STAR

Words and Music by Chad Kroeger,
Michael Kroeger, Ryan Peake and Daniel Adair

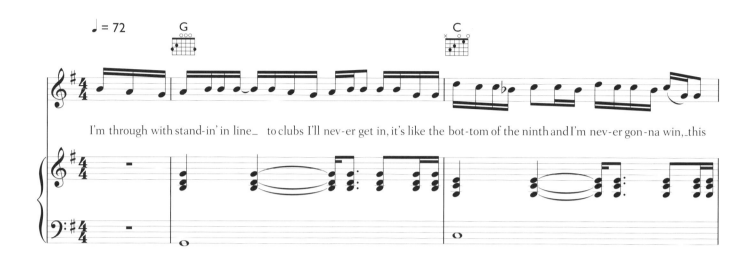

I'm through with stand-in' in line to clubs I'll nev-er get in, it's like the bot-tom of the ninth and I'm nev-er gon-na win, this

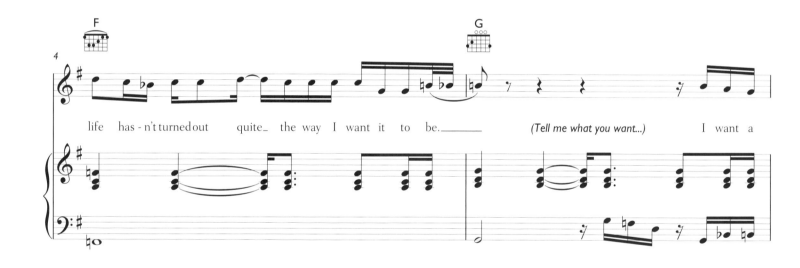

life has-n't turned out quite the way I want it to be. (Tell me what you want...) I want a

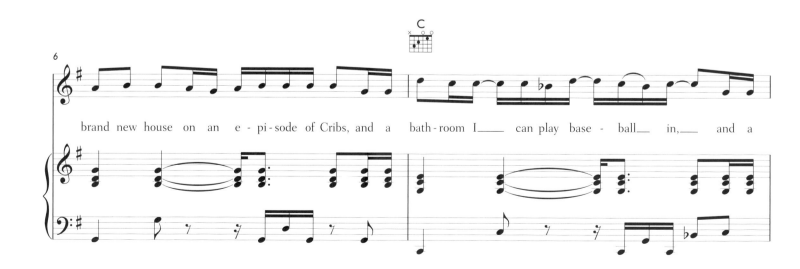

brand new house on an e-pi-sode of Cribs, and a bath-room I can play base-ball in, and a

155

STRANGE AND BEAUTIFUL

Words and Music by Matthew Hales and Kim Oliver

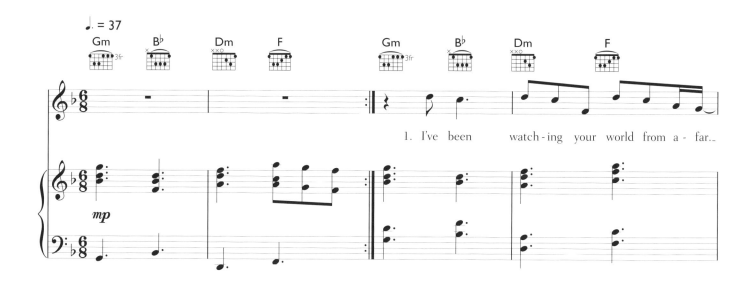

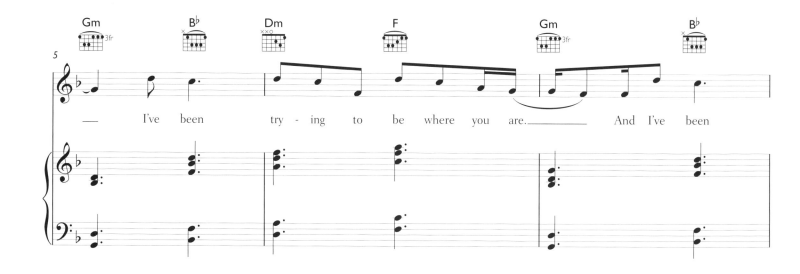

I'll be the first thing you see,____ and you'll re - a - lise____ that you love me.

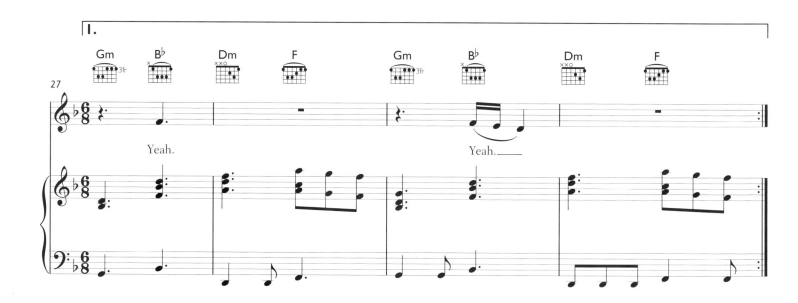

1.

Yeah. Yeah.____

2.

I'll put a spell on you, you'll fall a-sleep 'cause I'll put a spell on you,__ and when I wake you

I'll be the first thing you see,_____ and you'll re - a - lise___ that you love me, yeah.

Yeah.

Yeah._____

Fade

SWEET ABOUT ME

Words and Music by Gabriella Cilmi, Miranda Cooper,
Brian Higgins, Timothy Powell, Tim Larcombe and Nick Coler

163

SOUND OF THE UNDERGROUND

Words and Music by Brian Higgins, Niara Scarlett and Miranda Cooper

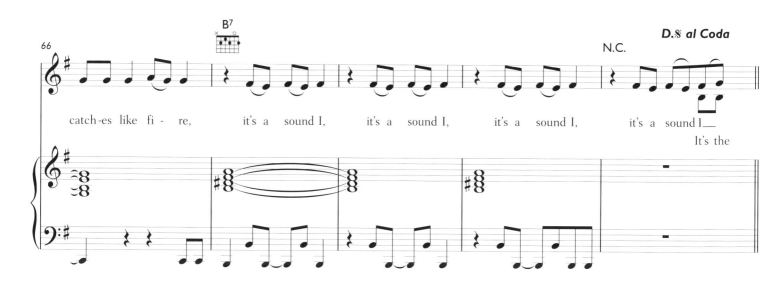

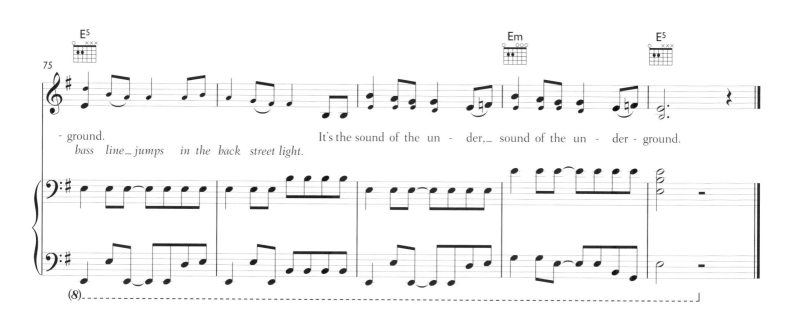

TALK

Words and Music by Guy Berryman, William Champion, Christopher Martin,
Jonathan Buckland, Karl Bartos, Ralf Huetter and Emil Schult

feel like___ a puz - zle, you___ can't find___ your mis-sing piece.___ Tell me

how_____ you feel._____ Well, I

feel like___ they're talk - ing in___ a lan - guage I don't speak,

___ and they're talk - ing it___ to me.___

THESE WORDS

Words and Music by Stephen Kipner, Andrew Frampton,
Natasha Bedingfield and Wayne Wilkins

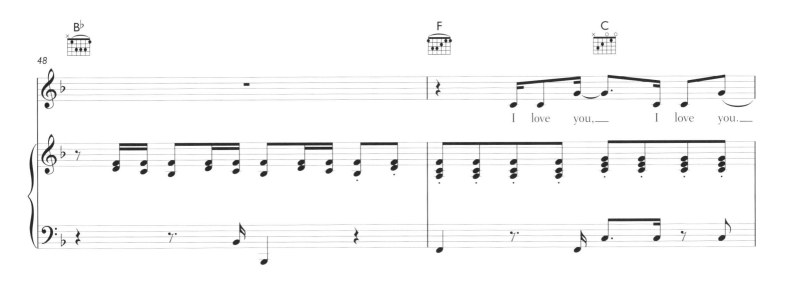

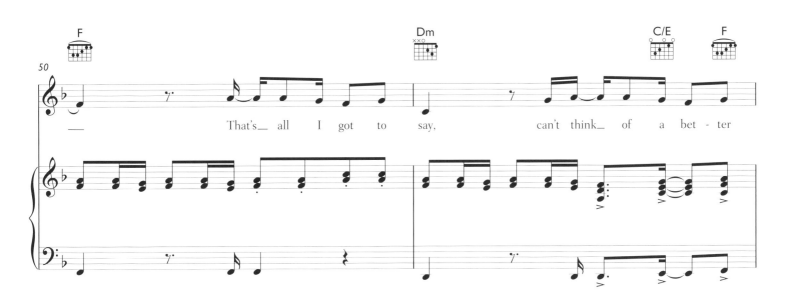

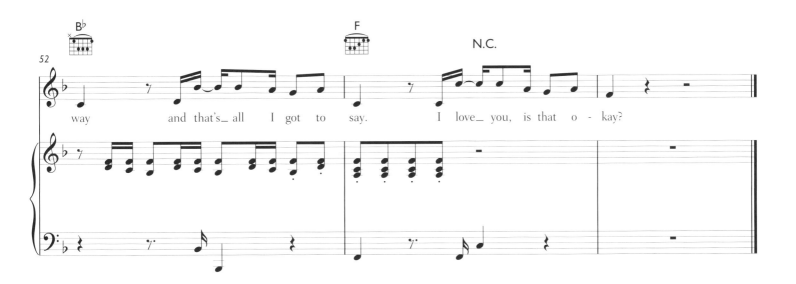

VALERIE

Words and Music by Dave McCabe, Sean Payne,
Abigail Harding, Boyan Chowdhury and Russell Pritchard

think of all the things___ what you're do - ing, and in my head___ I paint a pic-
did - n't catch a tan.___ Hope you found___ the right man___ who'll fix___ it
have to pay___ that fine___ you was dod - ging all the time? Are___ you still___

Play and repeat 2° only | I.3.4.

- ture.___
for___ you.___   3. Are you
bu - sy?___   'Cause

since I've come on home,___ well, my bo - dy's been___ a mess,___ and I miss

Green Day

WAKE ME UP WHEN SEPTEMBER ENDS

Words and Music by Billie Joe Armstrong, Michael Pritchard and Frank E. Wright III

wake me up___ when Sep - tem - ber ends.___

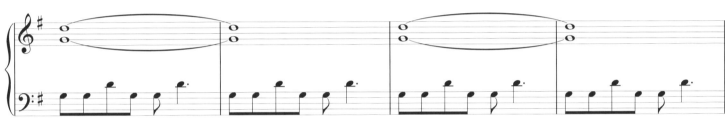

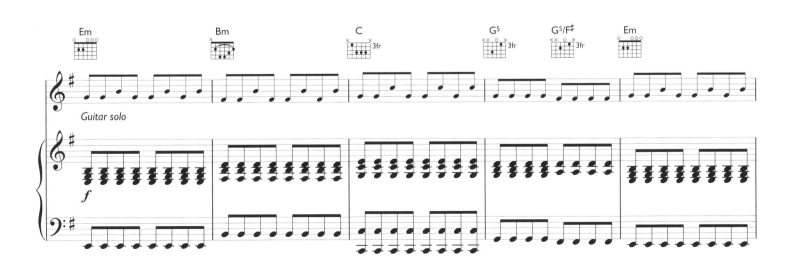

Guitar solo

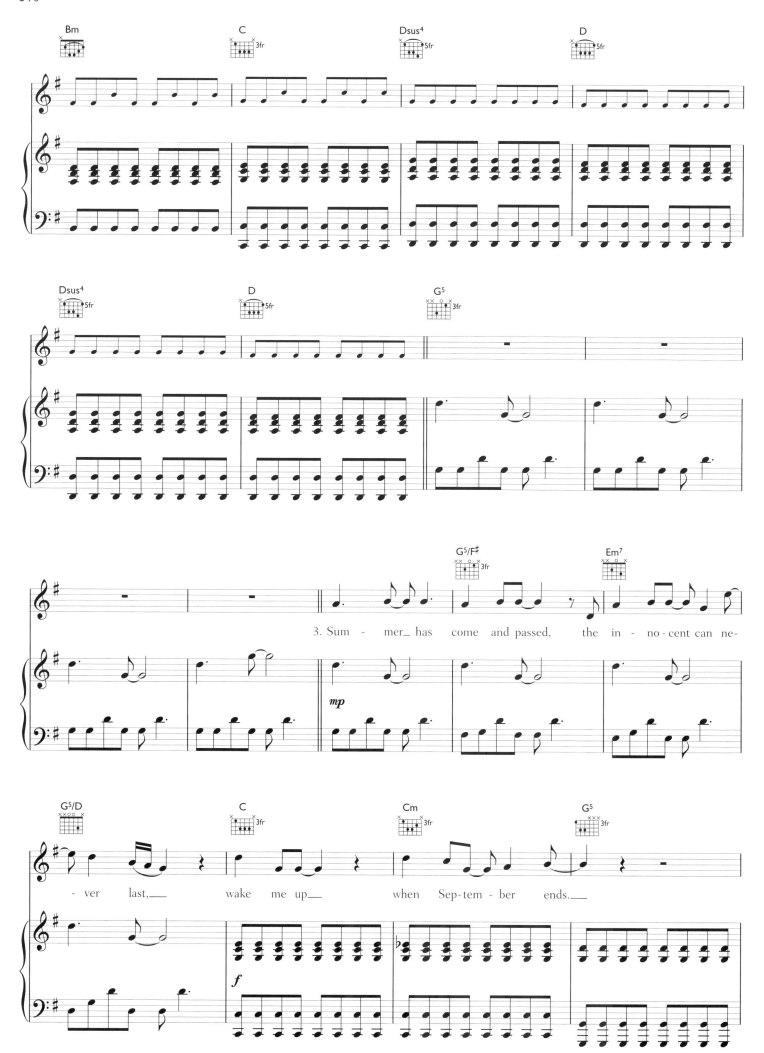

WARWICK AVENUE

Words and Music by Duffy, Jimmy Hogarth and Eg White

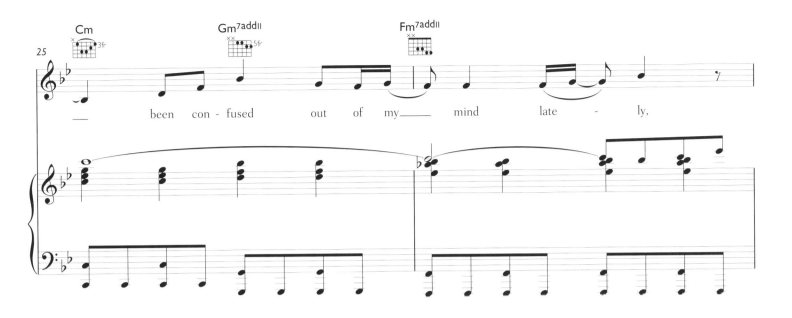

been con - fused out of my___ mind late - ly,

you_ think you're lov - ing__ but I want to__ be__ free,__ ba - by you've hurt__ me.__

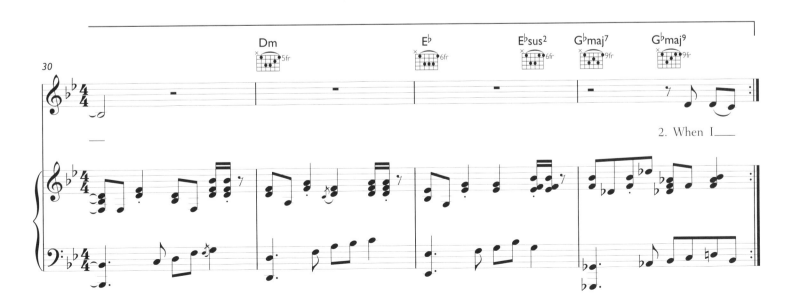

2. When I__

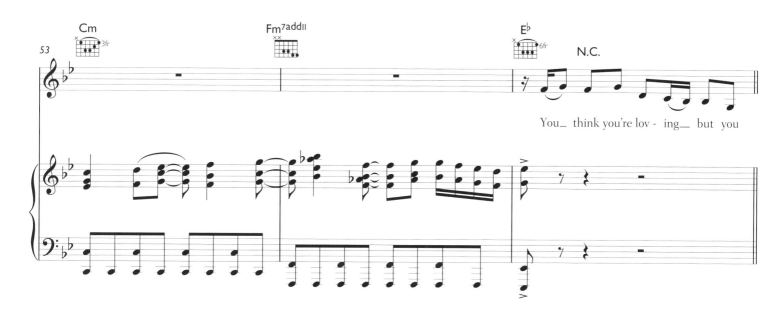

You_ think you're lov - ing_ but you

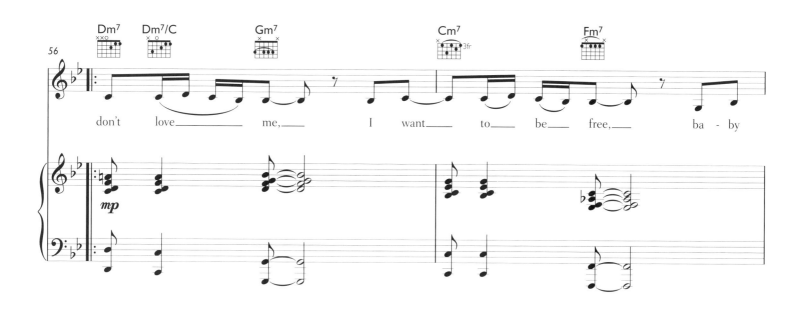

don't love_____ me,____ I want____ to____ be____ free,____ ba - by

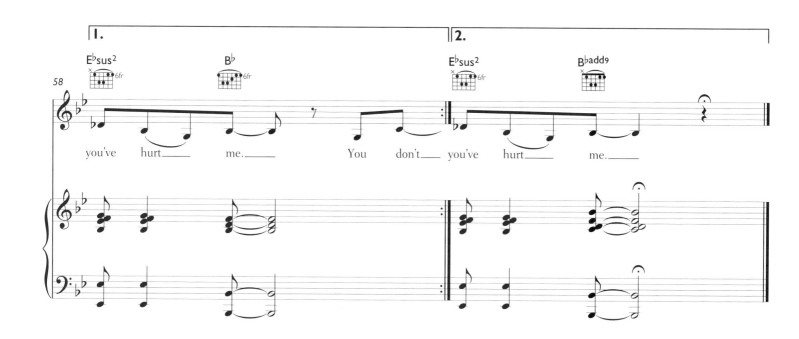

you've hurt____ me.____ You don't_ you've hurt____ me.____

YOU RAISE ME UP

Words and Music by Rolf Lovland and Brendan Graham

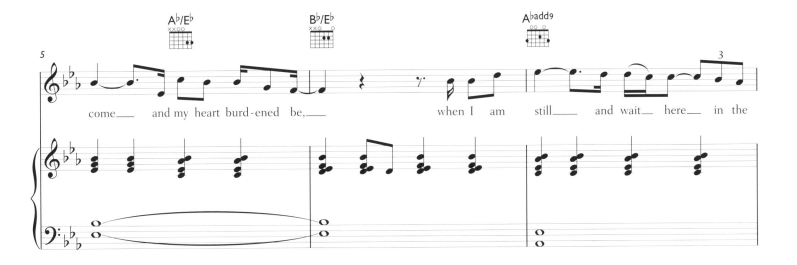

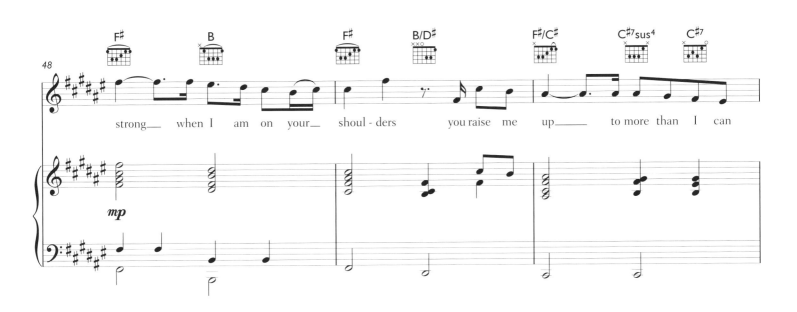

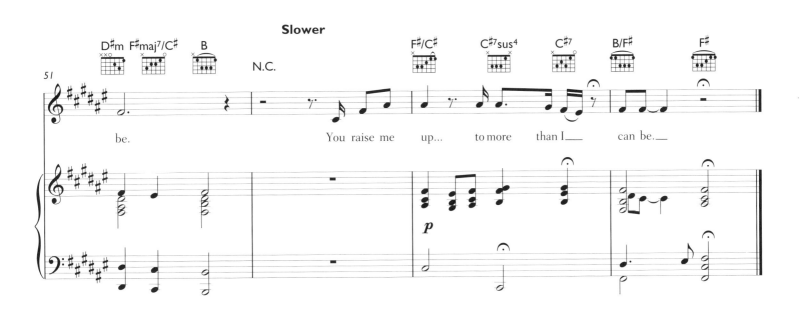

YOU'RE BEAUTIFUL

Words and Music by James Blunt, Sacha Skarbek and Amanda Ghost